# When Jackie Saved Grand Central

## The True Story of Jacqueline Kennedy's Fight for an American Icon

Written by **Natasha Wing**

Illustrated by **Alexandra Boiger**

HOUGHTON MIFFLIN HARCOURT
BOSTON   NEW YORK

WHEN JACKIE became First Lady of the United States in 1961, she moved into the White House with President John F. Kennedy and their children. The president's residence was the most famous house in the country—but Jackie was dismayed to find it as rundown as an old hotel. The walls needed painting, the furniture was shabby, and there were very few mementos of America's great leaders.

Like a history detective, Jackie tracked down lost presidential treasures—the desk used by Rutherford B. Hayes,

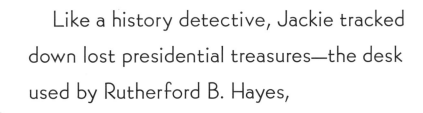

candelabras purchased by James Monroe,

a chandelier bought by Ulysses S. Grant.

Room by room, she restored the dreary mansion into a stately home that made Americans proud.

Fourteen years later, another famous landmark, this time in New York City, needed Jackie Kennedy's help . . .

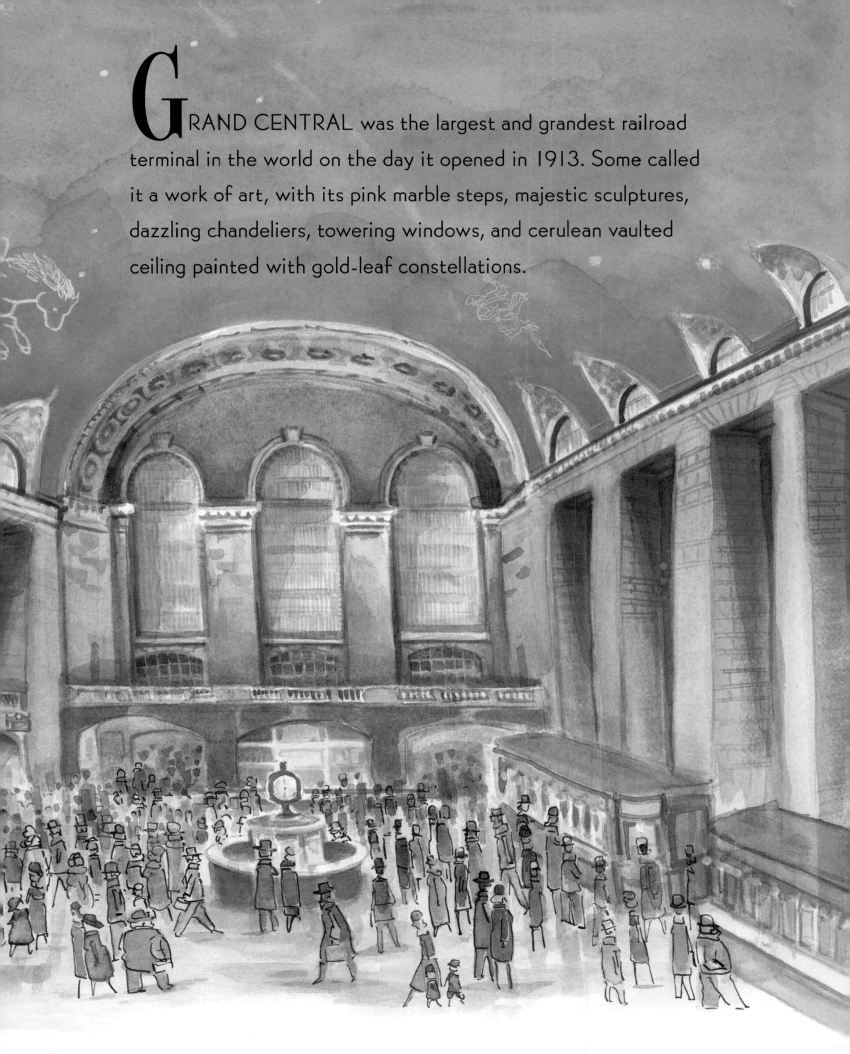

GRAND CENTRAL was the largest and grandest railroad terminal in the world on the day it opened in 1913. Some called it a work of art, with its pink marble steps, majestic sculptures, dazzling chandeliers, towering windows, and cerulean vaulted ceiling painted with gold-leaf constellations.

Over the years, Grand Central blossomed into the gateway to "the city that never sleeps." At the peak of train travel in the 1940s, it brought sixty-five million passengers in and out of New York City every year.

But it was more than just a place to pass through. Grand Central was where politicians gave speeches, movies were filmed,

revelers danced on New Year's Eve, and New Yorkers ate lunch.

Artist Andy Warhol even threw an underground party there.

Jackie had taken the train countless times
to and from Grand Central. It stood close to
where she had grown up on Park Avenue
and was at the heart of the glamorous city.
After her time in Washington, D.C., ended,
Jackie moved back to New York City to live
among the parks, museums, and magnificent
buildings she adored.

By the time Jackie returned, Grand Central had been at risk of losing its magnificence. Its owners wanted to build a skyscraper right on top of it. New Yorkers were outraged! Their historic building must be protected!

Luckily, the government agreed. The New York City Landmarks Law was enacted, giving the city a legal means to save its architecture. Grand Central was designated a landmark, and no one could change it. New Yorkers sighed in relief.

Yet Grand Central's owners were determined to build their skyscraper, so they filed a lawsuit with the State of New York. To the surprise of many, the judge ruled that the city was wrong to keep the owners from making money. He not only gave them permission to build their skyscraper—he said they could completely demolish Grand Central!

The *New York Times* ran a front-page story calling Grand Central "one of the most influential pieces of urban design of the twentieth century." Jackie read the article and couldn't believe what was happening. To her and many others, destroying Grand Central would be architectural mutilation.

When Jackie had renovated the White House, she realized how much Americans cared about their history. New Yorkers didn't want to lose this link to their city's past either. So Jackie wasn't going to let that happen.

Like a powerful locomotive, Jackie led the charge to preserve the landmark she and New York City loved. She joined city leaders and founded the Committee to Save Grand Central. She spoke at press conferences and made headlines.

She inspired citizens to donate money. When people across the United States saw their fashionable former First Lady championing her cause, New York City's fight became America's fight.

Jackie also wrote a letter to Mayor Abraham Beame,
saying, "Is it not cruel to let our city die by degrees,
stripped of all her proud monuments, until there is nothing
left of her history and beauty to inspire our children?"

She convinced the mayor to reject the court's decision and file an appeal. The campaign to save Grand Central would go back to court.

New York City won the appeal, as well as another that followed. New Yorkers cried, "No more bites out of the Big Apple!" It looked as if the beautiful Beaux Arts building would be saved once and for all.

But the fight wasn't over. The railroad owners took their case all the way to the U.S. Supreme Court, whose ruling would be absolutely final.

In a last-ditch effort to drum up support, Jackie boarded a special train called the Landmark Express. More than three hundred supporters joined her on the "whistle-stop crusade," traveling through stations in New York, Philadelphia, Wilmington, and Baltimore. Together they made tracks for Washington, D.C., hoping to gain attention for their cause in the place where the Supreme Court's decision would be made.

What a party the journey was! It was a
nonstop celebration of Grand Central!

Mimes,

musicians,

clowns,

and fire-eating jugglers performed
onboard. Volunteers handed out blue-and-white "Save Grand
Central" balloons, T-shirts, and buttons, while Jackie strolled
through the train cars, thanking fellow passengers personally.

When the Landmark Express pulled into Washington, fans and politicians swarmed Union Station to witness the return of the former First Lady to the nation's capital—and to demonstrate.

"If Grand Central Station goes," said Jackie to the press, "all of the landmarks in this country will go as well."

Jackie was worried. She had spent three years doing all she could to save Grand Central, yet the building's fate was now in the hands of the Supreme Court justices. This was the first time in history that the highest court in the nation had heard a case about historic preservation. It would not be an easy decision.

For two months, everyone anxiously waited.

Then, on June 26, 1978, the U.S. Supreme Court announced its ruling. The City of New York had won the case. Grand Central was saved! A victory for history!

One battle was over, but soon another would begin. How could the neglected Grand Central be brought back to its former splendor?

Architects studied original drawings and photos from the building's heyday and came up with a master plan, which Jackie enthusiastically supported.

It took almost two hundred million dollars and teams of craftsmen to get the job done. Nearly two decades passed before Grand Central shone once again.

And shine it did. New pink marble steps had been crafted. Sculptures at the grand Forty-Second Street entrance were restored.

Gold chandeliers had been stripped of their grime, and paint and dirt were removed from the towering windows. The interior was flooded with light once again. Even the ceiling, blackened from decades of soot and tobacco smoke, was carefully cleaned, revealing its cerulean color and golden constellations.

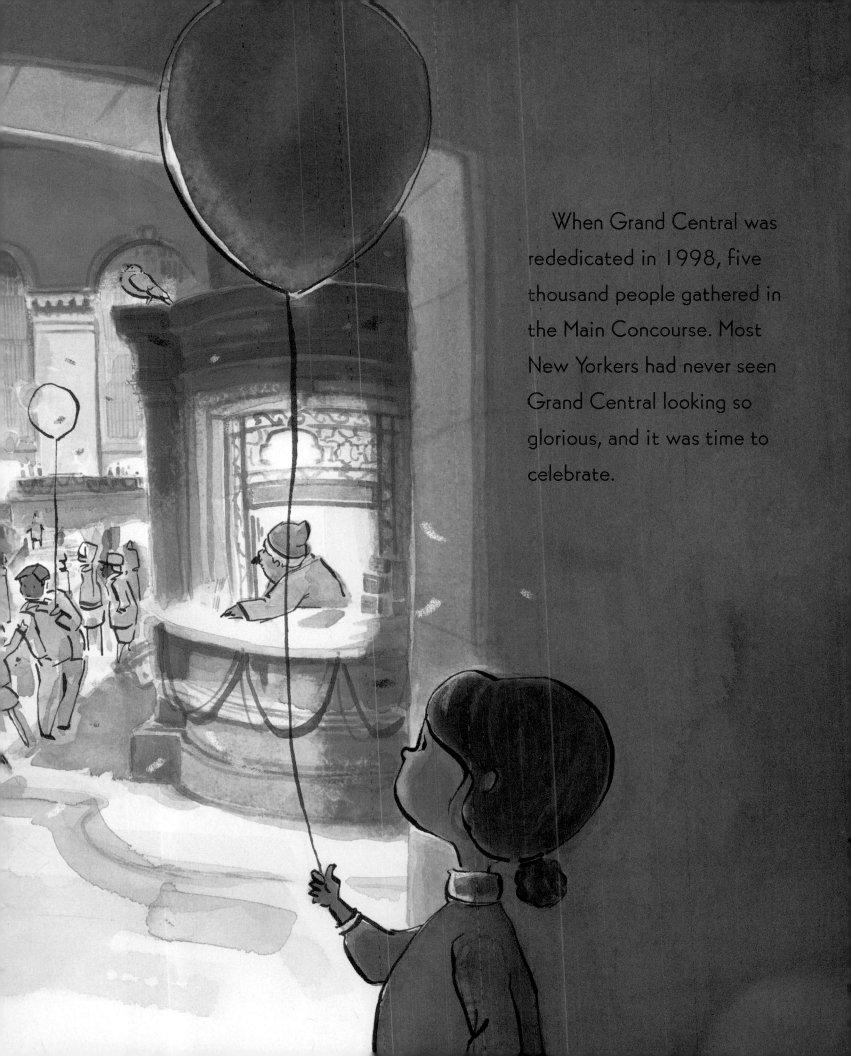

When Grand Central was rededicated in 1998, five thousand people gathered in the Main Concourse. Most New Yorkers had never seen Grand Central looking so glorious, and it was time to celebrate.

Yet one person was missing.

Jackie had died four years earlier. Many people honored her memory by visiting Grand Central to write messages in memorial books and linger in the beautiful space she had helped preserve. Today, Vanderbilt Hall and its entry foyer feature commemorations about Jackie so that no one will ever forget her role.

The fight to save Grand Central changed how people viewed old buildings. Rather than tearing them down, preservationists now had a model for how to save historic buildings all over the country, protecting our precious heritage.

Grand Central remains one of the grandest and most famous destinations in the world. Every day, it welcomes New Yorkers going to work, tourists visiting the sights, friends meeting for lunch . . . all because Jackie Kennedy and many others came together to save a landmark they loved.

# A Note from the Author

Jacqueline Kennedy once said that Grand Central Terminal "stands as a universal symbol between New York City's past and present."

In 1871, the first Grand Central Depot was built by railroad tycoon Cornelius Vanderbilt. The depot was rebuilt in 1899 and called Grand Central Station, the name many people still call it today. In 1913, the far larger Grand Central Terminal, much like we know it now, was completed. It is now the busiest stop of New York City's train system. About 750,000 people pass through Grand Central daily, and nearly twenty-two million tourists visit each year. With boutiques, restaurants, a food market, a museum, and many public events, the terminal has become a city within the city. The building wasn't saved just because it was pretty. Grand Central was restored so that it could be used again for the betterment of the city and its people. That's what preservation is all about: saving a building, a neighborhood, a park, or a landmark that represents our past so we can enjoy it in the present.

To Jackie, old buildings were also proud monuments, with history and beauty that could be an inspiration for children. She wondered, "If they are not inspired by the past of our city, where will they find the strength to fight for her future?" Her strong belief in preservation called her to action. She saved some important buildings that we still enjoy today, and her preservation efforts led to laws that have helped other people do the same where they live. Many have come to believe that if we fight to protect our past, our present and future will be richer.

Even before Jackie became the First Lady, she had a curiosity for the past and an appreciation for the arts. When she moved into the White House in 1961, she made it her mission to elevate the home to a showcase of presidential history and American art. Everything from wallpaper to chairs to dinnerware had to tie back to the history of the building and the people who occupied it. To help assemble and preserve White House artifacts, she established the Fine Arts Committee for the White House, and she later founded the White House Historical Association. In 1961, Congress passed a law that recognized that the museum character of the public rooms shall be preserved. Because of Jackie's vision, people today can tour the White House and learn about past presidents and the periods of history during which they served.

Jackie led preservation efforts beyond the walls of the White House, too. When the neighborhood across the street from the presidential residence was set for destruction to make way for modern court and office buildings, Jackie persuaded the developers to stop. She used her position as First Lady to get the plans changed. Old buildings were preserved rather than torn down, and new buildings were built to match the original architectural style. The restoration of the White House and the neighborhood of Lafayette Square led to the National Historic Preservation Act of 1966, which helps protect national heritage treasures. In 1970, Lafayette Square became a National Historic Landmark.

Back in New York City in the 1970s, Jackie became a leader in the battle to save Grand Central. Yet even after the Terminal's Supreme Court victory in 1978, there was more to be done for New York

City's buildings. Part of the historic St. Bartholomew's Church was at risk of being replaced with a fifty-nine-story office building. In 1984, Jackie rode her second Landmark Express train, which left Grand Central Terminal for New York's capital of Albany. At the hearing, she pointed out such examples as Notre Dame Cathedral in Paris as a reason to save houses of worship. The office tower was not built, and St. Bartholomew's landmark status remained.

After Jackie's death in 1994, the Municipal Art Society renamed its Presidents' Medal in honor of her dedication to preserve and protect New York City's architecture. The first Jacqueline Kennedy Onassis Medal recipient was Brendan Gill, who served with Jackie on the committee to save Grand Central Terminal. They and many other passionate Americans had been instrumental in saving an American icon for future generations.

# A Note from the Illustrator

When I looked up at the cerulean ceiling of Grand Central Terminal for the first time years ago, the bond I now feel with Grand Central and all of New York City was sealed. Illustrating this book was personal right from the start.

I used colors and symbols to highlight the emotional story line. The yellow birds represent the living, beating heart of Grand Central. The birds against the blue sky mirror the golden paintings on the ceiling inside the terminal. Birds also appear on national symbols, pointing toward the fight for justice and freedom. The people, collectively fighting to save Grand Central, come together in different tones of yellow. And Jackie herself, forever a part of Grand Central's history, is in yellow on the plaque placed in her honor near Vanderbilt Hall. Blue changes shades according to the mood. Black is used for the lawyers, the judges, and Jackie—those in powerful positions. Red is for highly dramatic situations, such as the anger, fear, power, and Jackie's protectiveness we encounter in the Supreme Court scene. It is significant that Jackie wears a red coat once she becomes actively engaged in the fight to save Grand Central.

Jackie's letter to the mayor was my compass to navigate through the events of this story. She used her eloquent voice when it really mattered.

# Selected Sources

Anthony, Carl Sferrazza. *As We Remember Her: Jacqueline Kennedy Onassis in the Words of Her Family and Friends.* New York: HarperCollins Publishers, 1997.

Belle, John, and Maxinne R. Leighton. *Grand Central: Gateway to a Million Lives.* New York: W. W. Norton & Company, 2000.

Nevins, Deborah. *Grand Central Terminal: City Within the City.* New York: Municipal Art Society of New York, 1982.

*To the people who continue the fight
to save and restore historic buildings*
—N.W.


*To my sister Margot, with love*

—A.B.


Thanks to Linda Pratt for planting the seed for this story; Jeannette Larson and Samantha McFerrin
for nurturing it with keen editing and support; Historic Preservation Consultant Kathleen P. Galop, Esq.,
for reviewing the many drafts for accuracy; the Municipal Art Society of New York City for research aid;
and Jacqueline Bouvier Kennedy Onassis for her passion for New York City's historic buildings.

—N.W.

• • ● ● ● • •

Text copyright © 2017 by Natasha Wing
Illustrations copyright © 2017 by Alexandra Boiger

www.hmhco.com

The illustrations in this book were done in watercolor, gouache, and ink on watercolor paper.
Spot colors and hand lettering were added digitally.
The text type was set in Bernhard Gothic.
The display type was set in Swashington.
Design by Christine Kettner

LIBRARY OF CONGRESS CATALOGING-IN-PUBLICATION DATA
Names: Wing, Natasha, author. | Boiger, Alexandra, illustrator.
Title: When Jackie saved Grand Central / by Natasha Wing ; illustrated by
Alexandra Boiger.
Description: Boston ; New York : Houghton Mifflin Harcourt, [2017]
Identifiers: LCCN 2016000983 | ISBN 9780547449210
Subjects: LCSH: Grand Central Terminal (New York, N.Y.)—Juvenile literature.
| Onassis, Jacqueline Kennedy, 1929-1994—Influence—Juvenile literature.
| Railroad stations—Conservation and restoration—New York (State)—New
York—Juvenile literature. | New York (N.Y.)—Buildings, structures, etc.
Classification: LCC NA6313.N4 W56 2017 | DDC 720.9747/1—dc23 LC record available at
https://lccn.loc.gov/2016000983

Manufactured in China
SCP 10 9 8 7 6 5 4 3 2 1
4500631441